# DOMENICO SCARLATTI

## THE SCHOLAR'S SCARLATTI

### A GRADED PROGRESSION OF 42 SONATAS THROUGH STYLE AND TECHNIQUE

### SELECTED AND EDITED BY STODDARD LINCOLN

### VOLUME ONE

WITH AN INTRODUCTION AND COMMENTARY,
AND NOTES ON THE INDIVIDUAL SONATAS

**NOVELLO
PUBLISHING LIMITED**
8/9 Frith Street, London W1D 3JB
Exclusive distributors: Music Sales Limited,
Newmarket Road, Bury St. Edmunds, Suffolk IP33 3YB

Order No: NOV100273

© Copyright 1989 Novello & Company Limited

All Rights Reserved    Printed in Great Britain

No part of this publication may be copied or reproduced in any form
or by any means without the prior permission of Novello & Company Limited

# Contents

| | |
|---|---|
| Foreword | page iv |
| Preface | v |
|     Introduction | v |
|     The Form and Structure of the Sonatas | vi |
|     Phrasing | vi |
|     Articulation and Touch | viii |
|     Trills | ix |
|     Appoggiaturas | xi |
|     Rhythm and Tempo | xii |
|     Fingering | xiii |
|     The Instrument | xv |
|     Sources | xvii |
| Table of signs and ornaments | xviii |

*Notes on the individual sonatas precede each set*

| | | |
|---|---|---|
| Set 1, F major: | K.274; L.297 | 1 |
| | K.85; L.166 | 4 |
| Set 2, G major: | K.289; L.78 | 6 |
| | K.35; L.386 | 8 |
| | K.425; L.333 | 10 |
| Set 3, D major: | K.335; LS.10 | 13 |
| | K.333; L.269 | 16 |
| | K.77; L.168 | 18 |
| | K.178; L.162 | 20 |
| Set 4, C major: | K.165; L.52 | 22 |
| | K.255; L.439 | 24 |
| Set 5, A major: | K.300; L.92 | 26 |
| | K.285; L.91 | 29 |
| | K.149; L.93 | 32 |

# Foreword

Stoddard Lincoln, who holds the highest degrees from the Julliard School of Music in performance and from Oxford University in music history, is the Dirctor of Graduate Studies at the Conservatory of Music at Brooklyn College and a Professor of Music on the Doctoral Faculty at the City University of New York. As a performer on both harpsichord and fortepiano he spends much time giving public concerts, coaching early music ensembles and lecturing. He has been a critic for *The Financial Times* (London) and is a staff reviewer for *Stereo-Review* where he specialises in writing about the early music scene.

His collection of Scarlatti sonatas combines excellent yet generally unfamiliar pieces with thorough technical and stylistic analyses. The sonatas have been chosen according to four criteria: the range of technical problems they present; the variety of styles and forms they contain; their musical quality; and their rarity (many being generally unavailable unless one purchases the complete works).

Professor Lincoln has also grouped the sonatas into Sets according to key. Each Set includes many different technical problems but also makes a satisfying musical unit for performance. Preceding each Set is a detailed commentary on the sonatas in the group, analysing the technical problems encountered, and suggesting approaches to the interpretation of each sonata. These commentaries on individual Sets are amplified by an extensive, informative Preface (only in Volume One), and a Table of signs and ornaments (to be found in each volume).

# Preface

## Introduction

The career of Domenico Scarlatti (1685-1757) is a singularly curious one. The son of Alessandro Scarlatti, the founder of Neapolitan opera and one of Italy's leading composers, Domenico's career got off to a promising start. After studies with his father he produced his first opera in Naples, continued his studies in Venice where he met Handel, and went to Rome where he was in the service of Queen Casimire of Poland, composing operas for her private theatre. After she left Rome he took a similar position with the Portuguese ambassador to the Holy See and also worked his way up to the post 'maestro di capella' at the Vatican.

Scarlatti was not only gaining a reputation as a composer, but also as a harpsichordist. When he met Handel in Venice, for example, the two were pitted against each other in a contest. Handel was honoured as the finer organist, and Scarlatti was recognized as the greater harpsichord player. Thus when he finally broke with his domineering father and went to Lisbon in 1719, he was not only given the post of 'maestro di capella' at the Royal Chapel, but he also became the music-teacher to the Princess Maria Barbara.

Although Scarlatti wrote music for the Royal Chapel, most of which was probably destroyed in the earthquake of 1755, his main interest seemed to be teaching and composing harpsichord music for his royal scholar. When she married the Spanish Crown Prince Fernando and moved to Madrid in 1728, Scarlatti went along as one of her retainers and seemed quite content to spend the remaining 28 years of his life in her service. The result of this felicitous relationship was some five hundred harpsichord sonatas of such beauty and originality that Scarlatti's reputation as a composer rests on this remarkable collection.

On reading through the sonatas, one is struck by the many passages that dwell on technical problems such as scales, arpeggios, trills, leaps, cross-hand work, double notes, and in fact, just about every technique required by a confidently-brilliant player. But such technical workouts are always so imaginatively woven into music of such high quality that one is not aware of their 'exercise'-like characteristics. Surely Scarlatti must have had his royal scholar in mind and made certain that Maria Barbara's training was thorough in both its technical and musical aspects.

Most collections of graded studies designed to develop technique are arid and not worth playing as music. The purpose of *The Scholar's Scarlatti* is to order a selection of sonatas in such a way that your technique will be developed in the context of fine music which is worth playing. You will become 'scholars' of Scarlatti and enjoy many of the same lessons that Maria Barbara worked on. Your training, like hers, will be thorough in both its technical and musical aspects.

Scarlatti's easiest sonatas, to be perfectly frank, are not really worth learning. One does much better with the easiest pieces of Bach and Couperin. Therefore, Volume One of *The Scholar's Scarlatti* does not begin with his easiest pieces, but rather with easy pieces and presents Scarlatti's basic technique at a moderate level. Volume Two continues exploring that technique at a moderately difficult level in more extended doses and also introduces leaps and cross-hand playing. Volume Three presents difficult works which sum up the technique. These sonatas are by no means Scarlatti's most difficult pieces. At this point, however, the scholar should be sufficiently equipped to tackle the most difficult virtuoso pieces and work out their demands confidently by himself.

In choosing this collection I have tried to avoid the popular sonatas and have chosen ones that are not usually found in other collections. On the other hand, if a popular sonata is the best presentation of a specific technical problem, it has been included.

Following the English eighteenth-century tradition, the sonatas have been arranged in *sets* according to key. While the *sets* become increasingly difficult, the individual sonatas of each *set* remain *at the same technical level*. Each *set* is planned as a musical unit so that it can be played in its entirety as a group in a recital and is preceded by a commentary which discusses the problems peculiar to each sonata in the *set*, such as fingering, phrasing, ornamentation etc.

## The Form and Structure of the Sonatas

A good interpretation of a piece of music must reflect its form and structure. Therefore it is necessary to understand how Scarlatti put his sonatas together. The vast majority of them are in a binary structure, i.e. the sonata is divided into two approximately equal sections. Usually each section is repeated, but this is up to the player. Not only is the binary structure articulated by the repeat signs, but also by its harmonic architecture. In most sonatas the first section modulates to the dominant if it is in a major key, or, if it is in the minor, it may modulate to the relative major rather than the dominant. The second section usually opens with a harmonic exploration, i.e. it goes through various keys, often including the relative minor of the tonic, and then finally settles down in the key of the tonic.

Within this structure, the form (the pattern of repetition) is greatly varied. In the vast majority of the sonatas, most of what happens in the first section is repeated in the second section, but not always in the same order or in the same key. In going through the sonatas, you will find some in which the second part is completely unrelated to the first part; there is a change in tempo and rhythm and it consists of all new material. One sonata inserts an unrelated minuet in the second part. Another contrasts tempo and material in both parts in an asymmetrical scheme. Scarlatti is also very fond of opening a sonata with a catchy tune for the right hand alone, then passing it along to the left hand as the right hand continues with a supporting line. However attractive this opening may be, it merely serves as a heraldic device never to appear again.

In a 'typical' sonata, Scarlatti likes to balance the two parts by closing them with the same material. It may only be four bars which may or may not be repeated immediately. Or it may be a series of ideas. Whatever these closing phrases may be, they terminate the first half in the key of the dominant (or relative major), and they are repeated at the end of the second section in the tonic. The point at which these repeated closing ideas in the second half begin is known as the 'crux' and is an important event in the form.

Understanding the form and structure of a Scarlatti sonata (and any Baroque or classical binary pieces, for that matter) has a direct application to learning the piece in hand. Harmonically, one is prepared for a modulation which creates tension in the first section as the tonality is pulled toward the new key. One should pay careful attention to any accidentals which will inevitably appear. In the opening of the second half one can expect even more tension because of the harmonic exploration and be doubly prepared for many more accidentals. The return to the tonic in the second half should come as a point of relaxation as one settles down into the opening tonality. Thus the harmonic architecture will help to scale the piece in terms of tension and relaxation.

The repetition of phrases in each half of a binary structure give unity to a sonata. Music which appears in both sections must be played the same way using the same phrasing and articulation. Usually, however, music that appears in one key in the first section will be in another key in the second section. In most cases it will have to be refingered, but it must sound the same. Thus a knowledge of the harmonic architecture of a binary structure and the recognition of phrases repeated in both sections is the key to a logical interpretation of a sonata.

## Phrasing

Amongst musicians it is the ability to phrase which separates the sheep from the goats. This means not only the knowledge to recognize a phrase, but, more important, to reveal that phrasing in one's performance. As a sentence is the basic unit or organisation in prose, so the phrase is the basic unit of organisation in music. Simply put, a phrase is a unit of music which achieves some sort of climax and then comes to some sort of repose. The climax need not be great, nor must the point of repose be complete, but the general rise to climax and fall to repose must be present.

Like classical composers, Scarlatti is fond of four-bar phrases, but, as is typical of Baroque composers, he often writes phrases of more than four bars and varies the phrase lengths for interest. One also finds very long phrases in Scarlatti which might encompass ten, twelve or even more bars.

Many of Scarlatti's phrases are stopped, that is, the point of repose is the final note of the phrase and the next note begins the new phrase. Phrases also may be separated by rests between them and sometimes (a great favourite with Scarlatti) a fermata or a full bar's rest. But Scarlatti is not always that clear in his separation of phrases: in order to keep the momentum of a piece going Scarlatti, like any good composer, will elide his phrases, a technique in which the last note of one phrase also serves as the first note of the next phrase.

While many modern editions use long, curved lines over a phrase to denote it, I have chosen to mark the ends of phrases with the upper part of a square bracket: ⌉ . This marking, I find, keeps the page cleaner looking and there is no confusion between it and markings for slurs and ties.

The necessity of breathing forces a singer to phrase as he coordinates his breathing with the phrasing. Keyboard players, on the other hand, are not dependent on breathing and can, and often do, simply play on and on without phrasing. This is boring to say the least. It is possible, however, to use the wrist for phrasing by starting a phrase with a low wrist and raising it until the end of the phrase. This, like all other techniques, takes thought, patience and careful practice.

A good way to begin learning the feeling of the rising wrist is to sit at a table about the same height as the keyboard and lay your fore-arm on it with your hand flat on the table. Now imagine that you are a marionette and that there is a string attached to the wrist. As the puppeteer, in your imagination, slowly pulls that string up, let your wrist rise ever so slowly keeping everything else completely relaxed. As the wrist rises it will eventually pull your hand up leaving it dangling, completely relaxed, in the air. After experimenting with this a few times, hold your fore-arm about an inch above the table with the hand spread out as it was when the table was supporting it. Hold this position for some time trying to keep your arm and hand steady. When you relax in this position your arm and hand will quite naturally fall to the table top. But do not let this happen – defy gravity! When you relax, let the wrist rise, as it did before, leading the hand upwards into the dangling position. The purpose of this exercise is to build up the association of rising, rather than falling, with relaxation.

If the image of the puppeteer does not work, try thinking that your fore-arm is floating in water and that the level of the water is slowly rising. Another useful image is to think of a napkin elegantly folded into the shape of a cone (as they do in some fancy restaurants). Try picking the napkin up by the tip of the cone as you naturally would without knocking it over. This produces a rather quicker movement than the other images, but the action of the wrist and hand position will be the same. Work on this motion over and over with both fore-arms until it is natural and easy.

Next, move to the keyboard and place your fingers, relaxed in a rounded position, on a C-major triad. Keep the wrist low (at the same level as the keys) and gradually raise it as you did at the table. Let that motion draw your fingers off the notes to a relaxed dangling position several inches above the keyboard. You might find it helpful to push the wrist up gently with your other hand. (Don't forget to try it with the left hand as well!)

Now we are ready for the exercise proper. With a relaxed hand, rounded fingers and a low wrist, play middle C with your second finger. Draw the wrist up as you have been doing and, as it is about to pull the second finger off C, play D with your third finger without releasing the C. As the wrist rises, allow it to draw the second and third fingers off C and D simultaneously. Continue up the keyboard using the second and third fingers on D and E, then E and F, and so on until you have reached the octave C. Take your time – don't rush! Now come down the octave reversing the action so that you begin with your third finger on C and take B with your second finger, still holding the C as you did coming up. When you are finished, let your arm hang loosely and gently shake out your hand.

Do the same with your left hand but in mirror motion. Play middle C with the second finger of the left hand and go down the octave using two and three, and then back up. Again dangle your arm and shake out the hand.

Returning to the right hand: do the same exercise with the third and fourth fingers, and the same in the left hand. After this, play the whole routine with the fourth and the fifth fingers of each hand. Don't forget to dangle your arm and shake the hand before shifting to the other hand.

Now play the same exercise beginning with your second finger on middle C, but this time as the wrist rises take D with the third finger, then E with the fourth finger, holding them all down until your wrist drags them off the notes. Precede up and down the octave as you did before, dangle and shake, and do the same with your left hand beginning with the second finger. You have probably guessed what happens next. Yes, do the same exercise with three, four and five in each hand, and finally use four fingers: two, three, four and five in each hand.

This exercise is time-consuming and requires infinite patience. It must, above all, be done slowly, and you must be constantly relaxed. Stick to it daily for at least a week, although it usually takes about a month for the technique to feel completely natural.

You will notice that no use has been made of the thumb. After a week you might try an octave scale on one wrist. Let the thumb hang naturally, keeping it relaxed, and pass it smoothly under the third or fourth finger as required by the scale.

At this point you might try some phrases from the sonatas in this volume hands separately using the rising wrist action. The opening phrase of the first sonata (K. 274 in F Major) is a good example. Play the first five bars trying out the rising wrist. Then take bars five to ten for the left hand alone. Sonatas 6 and 7 are also good ones to try the same way. Make sure that your wrist rises until the end of the phrase, and repeat it over and over until the phrase becomes an automatic gesture of the wrist.

The results of this exercise will not be immediately perceptible, but with enough practice the use of the wrist for phrasing will become second nature. In long phrases you will find it impossible to keep constantly raising the wrist, but the mere thought of its raising will hold the phrase together. In the long run, however, coordinating the wrist with phrasing will enhance your playing more than any finger exercises will ever do.

## Articulation and Touch

As a sentence is subdivided into clauses, so a phrase is subdivided into fragments or motifs. In this edition articulation is marked by the use of a comma (,). In playing, it is marked by the slightest break which is done by a minute shortening of the note before the articulation sign. Say you are playing a C-major scale in crotchets (quarter notes), for example, and there is an articulation sign between G and A; you would play the G as a dotted quaver (eighth-note) followed by a semiquaver (sixteenth-note) rest. The A would be slightly accented. The wrist maintains the rising motion taking the entire scale as one phrase, and the fingers do the articulation without disturbing the wrist movement. In other words, the wrist is used for phrasing and the fingers for articulation.

Articulations that are called for in rapid passage work scarcely give the player time to make an actual break as described above without disturbing the flow of the run. In this case simply accent the note after the articulation.

In playing Baroque melodies, and many classical as well, there are certain articulations that are taken for granted and are not marked in the score. The two principal ones involve dotted notes and ties. Dots are read as rests. If, for example, you have a dotted minim (half-note) followed by a crotchet (quarter-note), you play a minim, a crotchet rest (the value of the dot) and then the final crotchet note. Likewise, if you have a dotted quaver (eighth-note) followed by a semiquaver (sixteenth-note) you play a quaver, a semiquaver rest (the value of the dot) and then the semiquaver note – all, of course, within the phrase.

If there is a tie you treat the second note of the tie as a rest. For example, if you have a crotchet (quarter-note) tied to the first of a group of four semiquavers (sixteenth-notes), you play the crotchet, read the first semiquaver note as a rest and then play the three remaining semiquaver notes.

Articulations are also used before any notes on offbeats which are quicker than the note or notes they follow. For example, if you have a crotchet on the first beat followed by two quavers or four semiquavers on the second beat, you make a tiny articulation before the second beat.

Baroque melodies and figurations are made up of many small fragments. Many times these fragments are motifs which give unity to the melodies or figurations. Articulation with the fingers brings out the motifs and prevents them from running into each other in an aimless line. Phrasing with the wrist holds them all together in a basic shape. It is like a necklace: the pearls and diamonds are the articulations and the cord which holds them together and gives them their shape and function is the phrase.

Touch is closely akin to articulation. There are three touches: legato, staccato and slurred. Legato is the normal, work-a-day touch that one normally uses, and even within legato there is room for slight variation. In the most common type of legato one note is released as the other is played with no overlapping of sound. In passage work where brilliance is desired, there can be a tiny, tiny space between the notes, but not enough to make it staccato. This type of legato gives a sheen to passage work and brings out its brilliance. Legato is not marked in a score, but taken for granted when there is no other marking.

Staccato playing involves striking the notes smartly and holding them for half their written value. This is indicated by a dot over the note.

Slurred notes are held so that the sound overlaps slightly. If one is confronted with two slurred crotchets, the second is played before the first is released. Slurred notes that outline chords may be held down so that all of the notes of the chords will eventually resonate together. Slurring is indicated by a slur or arched line over the notes.

All of these touches are used within the phrase. As in articulation it is the finger that makes the touch, not a wrist motion. That is reserved *at all times* to control the phrase.

Markings for articulation and touch are given the first time a motif or figure appears. The same articulation *must* be used each time the motif reappears no matter what key it is in or how varied. In the first sonata, for example, the trill-like figure on the second and third beats of bar 11 is used throughout the piece. They must always be articulated as initially indicated. Likewise, the slurs from the second beat of bar 14 to the first beat of bar 15 should also be applied from the second beat of bar 15 to the first beat of bar 16, and so on. The contrary motion scales found in the second half of the sonata (bars 37–39 and 41–43) must also be played the same way.

All marks indicating phrasing, articulation and touch are editorial. Exceptions are mentioned in the commentary to the individual sonatas.

## Trills

While France and Germany evolved a fairly precise system of ornamentation and have left us with many treatises describing it, Italy left ornamentation to the performer, indicated little more than trills and left almost nothing in the way of explanatory documents. Coming from the Italian tradition and being somewhat isolated in Spain, Scarlatti's ornamentation is sparse and vague. Although many experts on the subject of ornamentation have tried to apply the principles of the Franco-Germanic school to Scarlatti, his music is so different that the principles that apply to such composers as Bach and Couperin are musically unsatisfying when applied to Scarlatti. The best plan, then, is to examine Scarlatti's ornamentation in its own right without reference to his contemporaries in France, Italy and Germany.

A perusal of the earliest printed and written sources teaches us that Scarlatti used two signs: **Tr** and ⁓. A comparison of different sources for the same sonata reveals the uncomfortable fact that the signs were used interchangeably: a **tr** in one source will be ⁓ in another source. Inconsistencies are even found within the same source as repeated passages are often written out identically but use different trill signs. Therefore, there is no point in trying to differentiate between them and for our purposes, then, they are all trills.

As a general rule, Baroque and classical trills begin on the upper auxiliary, i.e. the note above the written note, as in Example 1A.

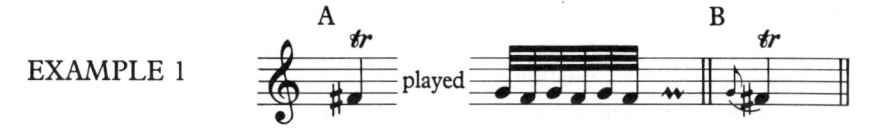

EXAMPLE 1

Scarlatti frequently writes a grace note before a trill, as in Example 1B, which leaves no doubt that he wants it to begin on the upper auxiliary. The implication is that a trill without a grace note begins on the principal note. Realising that ornamentation in the Baroque era was frequently a matter of the performer's personal taste, one must conclude that a trill in Scarlatti can begin either on the principal note or on the upper auxiliary, but that when he wants it to begin on the upper auxiliary he precedes it by a grace note.

In this edition the fingering will tell you whether to use an upper auxiliary or not. In the right hand, if a trill on F is indicated by the fingering **23** or **34**, it begins on the principal note. If it is fingered **32** or **43**, it obviously begins on the upper auxiliary. These are of course, only suggestions, and you are free to experiment with the first note. When Scarlatti precedes a trill by a grace note, I have left it so that you can tell that here Scarlatti really wants the upper auxiliary and that you are not free to experiment. All trills are fingered in this edition.

Trills frequently include a termination, i.e. the antipenultimate note of the trill is a step below the written note as in Example 2A.

EXAMPLE 2

When Scarlatti really wants this he writes it out, as in Example 2B. Again, the implication is that when Scarlatti really wants a termination, he writes it out. If he does not, the use of a termination is left to the discretion of the performer.

Another problem Scarlatti does not address is how long a trill should be. Should it be long and occupy the entire beat, or should it be short and occupy only part of the beat?

In this edition I distinguish between the 'long' trill which occupies the entire beat, and the 'short' trill which takes only part of the beat, by assigning two different readings to the two signs Scarlatti used and using those signs consistently. Example 3A is a long trill and 3B is a short trill.

EXAMPLE 3

Even though these examples begin on the upper auxiliary, remember that they could just as well begin on the principal note, F sharp.

Take careful note that the long trill always has a termination and that the short trill does not. The reason for this is, in my mind, a musical one. In these examples, the trills are on F sharp and resolve to G. The note of resolution after a trill must be clearly distinguished, or articulated, from the trill proper or the listener will be frustrated and not know where he is. In Example 4, the long trill goes directly from the F sharp to the G and it sounds as though the trill simply stops mid-stream without a satisfactory resolution. This is because the function of the G as the note of resolution has not been distinguished from the function of G as a member of the trill. This difference in function as trill member and as note of resolution must somehow be made clear to the listener. By using a termination, as in example 3A, the listener is signalled by the sudden dip to E that the next time he hears G it will be the note of resolution. It is also articulated by time. During the trill proper the G sounds on every semiquaver. By substituting an E for the last one of those Gs, the final G's function as the note of resolution is clearly heard because it is spaced further down the time-stream than the preceding Gs of the trill.

In the short trill the double function of the G is heard because there is a pause between them. This pause is enough – there is no need of a termination.

The short trill, especially one beginning with an upper auxiliary, is used for brilliance. Played quickly, they add sparkle to a note. They are usually used within the phrase. You should always try to stop on the last note of the trill before proceeding to the next note, but in rapid passages this can be all but impossible.

At times, it is technically very difficult to fit in all the notes required by a short trill beginning with the upper auxiliary. In such a case begin the trill on the principal note regardless of what I have recommended in the fingering. You will have no trouble with short trills between the strong second and third fingers. Short trills between the third and fourth fingers, however, can be bothersome, especially if the upper note is an accidental. If you cannot negotiate the upper auxiliary, omit it. But this is a stop-gap until you have built up your technique to the point where you can negotiate them.

Besides the technical reasons given above, trills beginning on the principal note are often used to achieve smoothness when the trill is preceded by its upper neighbour.

The long trill is usually reserved for important cadences at the ends of phrases. It is all but obligatory at the final cadence of a sonata and at the cadence of the first section before the first repeat sign.

In lyric melodies trills should be played expressively as part of a vocal line rather than for brilliance. A good way to achieve this effect is to linger on the first note of the trill whether it be the upper auxiliary or the principal note. Then go into the trill with a slight accelerando but never reaching the speed that you would apply to a trill for brilliance. In slow-moving melodies there might be time for more notes in a short trill than the four indicated in Example 3B. Play as many as you wish, but just make certain that you pause on the last note before moving to the resolution. If you extend a short trill which is over a dotted note, stop the trill at the dot, i.e. a short trill over a dotted crotchet followed by a dotted quaver will stop on the third quaver, as in Example 4B. Remember that if the fingering were **34**, the trill would begin on B and the number of notes in it adjusted accordingly.

EXAMPLE 4

Scarlatti loves to repeat short motifs containing trills and will do it as many as four times in succession. Using the same trill for each repetition is boring. Vary them. Begin some on the upper auxiliary and some on the principal note. Hold the first note longer in some than in others. Experiment and make the trills sound improvised.

## Appoggiaturas

An appoggiatura is a dissonance or non-chord tone which moves up or down a step to its note of resolution. It is indicated by a small note before the note of resolution and the stem of the appoggiatura goes up no matter where it falls on the staff. A written slur usually connects the two.

In going through the original sources of the Sonatas, one finds appoggiaturas of all note values gracing notes of all values in every conceivable rhythmic combination, a few of which are given in Example 5.

EXAMPLE 5

In comparing the appoggiaturas of the same sonata in different sources there are many discrepancies in their written value. Discrepancies also appear within a single sonata from the same source, and one is apt to find repeated passages which are written out identically but use different appoggiaturas in the same place. One concludes that Scarlatti used them as inconsistently and as capriciously as he did the trill.

While the French and Germans left many treatises on the length of appoggiaturas, the Italians left very few, and what Scarlatti did in Spain is questionable. Experts have tried to apply the Franco-Germanic tradition to Scarlatti, but it rarely works.

For the purposes of *The Scholar's Scarlatti*, I have again taken the bull by the horns and imposed consistent usage on how the length of appoggiaturas is indicated.

The term appoggiatura means to lean and its purpose is to stress a dissonance or non-chord tone. This is done by articulation and touch. Always make a slight articulation before an appoggiatura and then slur it to the note of resolution, i.e. do not release the appoggiatura until after you have played the note of resolution.

In this edition, all appoggiaturas are held for their written value, and that value is subtracted from the note it graces. Here are a few examples:

EXAMPLE 6

Appoggiaturas are always short before triplets, repeated notes and syncopations. Like short trills, they are used for brilliance and often function to accent a note. Long appoggiaturas are used melodically in order to stress a dissonance or non-chord tone, as described above.

A very special kind of appoggiatura is the acciaccatura. It is written as a quaver appoggiatura with a slash across the tail ♪. It is played as quickly as possible: so quickly, in fact, that more frequently than not it is played simultaneously with the note it precedes. If you play the acciaccatura at the same time you play the principal note release the acciaccatura immediately so that one hears the principal note clearly.

Acciaccaturas may be substituted for short trills when it is technically impossible for you to negotiate the trill as indicated. This means that you do not have to give up playing a sonata which has an impossible trill in it. But substituting an acciaccatura for that trill is only temporary until you have sufficient technique to play the trill properly.

In listening to many performances of Scarlatti you will hear a lot of long appoggiaturas based on the Franco-Germanic tradition of holding them, regardless of how notated, for half the length of the note of resolution and for two-thirds of it if the note is dotted. At the present time, this reading of Scarlatti's appoggiaturas is under fire, and a shorter reading of them is favoured. I have found that the length of an appoggiatura as Scarlatti wrote it is usually very effective, but there are times when his usage is wildly inconsistent. Any changes I have made, then, are for the sake of consistency.

**Rhythm and Tempo**

French music, and possibly some German music written in the French style, makes use of rhythmic alterations, a tradition in which notes written in equal time values are played in unequal time values. This does not apply to the Italian tradition and, thank heavens, Scarlatti is Italian. I mention this because at some time or other you are bound to come across French rhythmic alterations and, in your enthusiasm, you might be tempted to apply them to Scarlatti. Don't! Such an application is completely misguided.

This by no means implies that Scarlatti's music, or any music for that matter, should be played metronomically in strict rhythm. One should, of course, practise with a metronome to make sure that one has a basically steady pulse throughout an entire piece, but then it must be loosened up.

Today we are accustomed to making our expression through dynamics: crescendos, diminuendos, sudden contrasts in *forte* and *piano*, and accents. This was impossible in Scarlatti's day, at least for the keyboard, and instead expression was achieved by temporal means (ritardandos, accelerandos, tempo rubato and agogic accents) and the beat, to a certain extent, was flexible.

The most obvious temporal deviation, and one still widely practised today, is the ritard. Although many musicians reserve ritardandos for the final cadence only, there is no reason whatsoever why they should not be applied to the cadence of the middle half *and* the final cadence of a sonata. Ritardandos in Baroque music should not be grandiose affairs spanning several measures. A slight slowing down of the tempo on the last few beats before the cadence will suffice. Naturally, a lyric piece will take more ritard than a fast brilliant one.

In flashy bravura sonatas, a ritardando will often kill the brilliance and take the starch out of the cadence. At the same time, one cannot go crashing into the final note or chord without some sort of warning signal to the listener. In such cases an agogic accent is effective. One simply makes an articulation (a miniscule space) between the penultimate and final notes. Simply think of taking a catch breath before the last note.

Ritardandos are also used within the body of a sonata as well as at the two cadences. A fermata or a bar's rest are both prepared by ritardandos. Without them, it sounds as though one suddenly hits a wall at full force, an extremely undesirable effect. Ritardandos may also be used judiciously to mark important inner cadences. But here one must use extreme caution and they are best avoided when first learning a piece.

Extremely important is the use of rubato. Rubato means that the beat is 'robbed'. This is done by means of slight accelerandos, ritardandos and hesitations. Rubato is applied mostly to lyric passages in sonatas. If there is a particularly poignant dissonance in a melody, one wants to savour it by lingering on it slightly. When taking a high note preceded by a large leap, take your time as a singer would. A particularly delicious chord progression or a sudden shift to the minor should also be savoured by a slight ritard. In expressive passages, appoggiaturas, always dissonant, should be subtly held, or as the term implies, leaned on. If a rising melodic line changes its direction for a descent, one wants to mark that change of direction by a slight ritardando just before the highest note, to get one over the hump, so to speak. And then begin the descent slowly, gradually returning to the original tempo.

In convoluted passages, such as a descending run of broken thirds mingled with other intervals, one might want to give the effect of unfolding the music – presenting it like a flower revealing its beauty as it blooms. Begin the run slowly and gradually pick up the tempo until you return to the original.

In quick and brilliant sonatas tempo rubato is infrequent as it kills their dash, but there is a place for a limited amount. In triple time, where a strong downbeat is desirable, the downbeat can be emphasized by holding it slightly. Exciting passages may surge forward a bit. But remember, no matter what the basic tempo of a piece is – be it *adagio* or *allegro* – one must always return to that basic tempo. This is why it is advisable to start working with a metronome; it will instill the basic pulse in your system so that you can always return to it.

Rubato must be used with such subtlety that it is scarcely perceptible. The listener should not be so much aware of your rhythmic deviations as of your expressiveness and musicality. It is impossible to indicate rubato in a score and indications of ritardandos are hazardous at best. The latter are easily worked out. A few passages requiring rubato are discussed in the commentary.

Characteristic of Baroque music in triple time is the ubiquitous hemiola. In 3/8 time, for example, one normally accents the first beat, as in Example 7A.

EXAMPLE 7

Scarlatti and his contemporaries, however, are very fond of creating excitement at cadence points by accenting every other beat: ONE, two, THREE, one, TWO, three, as seen in example 7B. In this edition hemiolas are marked in the left hand with brackets, as seen in Example 7C. Once you have become aware of them you will spot them all over the place in all Baroque composers and enjoy their excitement.

In most cases, Scarlatti heads his sonatas with an Italian tempo marking. In the Baroque era, however, the words were taken for their literal meaning, not relative tempos to each other as our modern metronome implies. *Allegro* meant happy, not fast. *Andante* meant walking, not slow. *Adagio* meant at ease, not very slow. Thus a Baroque composer was apt to come up with such seemingly contradictory markings as *andante allegro* (walking happily), or *andante adagio* (walking at ease).

More important than establishing a tempo in a Baroque piece is determining its 'affection', or mood. Is it happy, sad, angry, stately or whimsical? Is it a march, a dance or a song? This, of course, can be a very personal matter, but thinking of the actual meaning of the Italian will help you to start thinking about the affection.

In this edition I have offered metronome markings. Initially, you will begin far below them until the technical problems are sorted out and then gradually move to that marking. Remember, however, that these markings are only suggestions and, while they fit my purposes, they might not suit you. Eventually you will set your own tempos remembering two things: are you technically secure at that tempo? and can one hear all that is going on in the music at that tempo?

## Fingering

Many aspects of fingering are so obvious that they are taken for granted. Focusing on the obvious, nonetheless, solves many problems which are not even recognized if the obvious is always taken for granted. These observations on fingering, then, are mostly obvious, but thinking about them is helpful and will clarify how I have chosen and indicated fingering in this edition.

The most important thing about fingering is not to improvise it as you go along. Sooner or later you will come to grief as you run out of fingers and there is one note left to go, or you crack up against an accidental with your thumb when you least expect it. Such accidents are not only gauche, but can be extremely embarrassing. Learn the fingering of a piece the same way you learn the notes and rhythm. As the notes and rhythm must be the same, so must the fingering. Learning a piece is simply building up a habit; fingering must be part of that habit. If you come across fingering that does not fit your hand – and all hands are different – write in any changes you make. If you are learning a piece which has no fingering, finger it first. As you begin to work up speed, you might find that you want to make further changes to fit your hand better. Write those changes in before you forget them and before your fingers falter in the passages when you come to them. Fifty-per-cent of learning a piece is using the same fingering at all times. Fifty-per-cent of technique is using the correct fingering.

As for reading fingering, obviously, consecutive fingers are used for consecutive notes in conjunct motion and the fingering will tell you which finger to begin with. Using the thumb on accidentals, while not strictly forbidden, is discouraged because of the awkward position it creates in the hand and the lumpiness it is apt to produce in an otherwise smooth passage. In order to avoid placing the thumb on an accidental, you must be careful where you pass the thumb under. Beginning an ascending F-major scale with the right hand thumb, for example, you must pass the thumb under the fourth finger on B flat and play it on C.

### EXAMPLE 8

If you were to pass the thumb under the third finger on A, you would have to hoist the whole hand up to play the thumb on B flat. Such an awkward motion would interfere with the rising wrist and destroy the phrase. The fingering in this edition indicates the placement of the thumb when it passes under in order to avoid ending up with the thumb on an accidental.

Beginning a descending F-major scale with the fourth finger the thumb will be on C and the fourth finger should pass over it and take the B flat so that one can continue right down to the thumb on F. (See Example 8B.) If one passes the third finger over the thumb for the B flat, one will end up a note short with the thumb on G and have to pass another finger over the thumb to get to the final F. By crossing the fourth finger over rather than the third, however, you have enough fingers to get to the final destination wthout having to do another cross-over. Therefore, I have indicated which finger to cross over the thumb.

If you have the notes C and E in your right hand, it is normal to take the C with the thumb and the E with the third finger, or the C with the second finger and the E with the fourth, and so on. Occasionally it is necessary to take the C with the thumb and the E with the second finger rather than the third. This is known as an expansion. If, in Example 8C, you take the E with your third finger, you will wind up with your fifth finger on G and still have to get to the A somehow. By taking the E with your second finger you will have enough fingers left to get there. I have given the fingering for such expansions.

A contraction is when you have two conjunct notes but skip a finger: C/D, fingered one/three, or two/four. If in Example 9A you took the F sharp with your second finger and descended from the G beginning with the third finger, your thumb would land on E and you would have to get to D by hook or by crook.

EXAMPLE 9

The contraction between E and F sharp, however, allows you to begin the descent with the fourth finger so that you can arrive at the D easily without another cross-over. Contractions are indicated in the fingering.

Fingerings in the seventeenth and early eighteenth centuries favoured crossing short fingers over long fingers and almost complete avoidance of the thumb, as seen in Example 9B, a little exercise (*Applicatio*) Bach wrote out and fingered for his eldest son. As the century wore on, however, the thumb came into use and gradually passing the thumb under became acceptable. One can only surmise how Scarlatti fingered his music, but considering how 'modern' his keyboard writing is for its day, one can guess with a certain amount of accuracy that he used the thumb as we do today. There are times, nonetheless, when it is convenient to cross fingers over each other. Such a passage is seen in Example 10A.

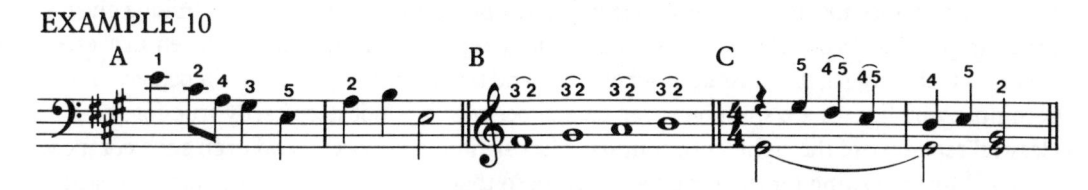

EXAMPLE 10

You could, of course, put the thumb on A and the second finger on G sharp making a contraction to the fifth finger on E. Considering that this is the end of a phrase and your wrist is rising, crossing the third finger over the fourth comes naturally and helps the rising wrist action.

We are all too apt to forget about crossing fingers over, but there are times when it is a life-saver. I have suggested some of these times in the fingering.

Changing fingers on repeated notes, especially rapid ones, is essential. Scarlatti himself mentions it. This is indicated in the fingering the first time it occurs, **4321** over four semiquaver As, for example. When such a figure is constantly repeated, I have only indicated the finger to begin with.

Substituting fingers on held notes is equally important for slurred passages and for melodies in which you do not want a break. You might practise ascending and descending scales substituting fingers as in Example 10B but using all combinations (**23, 34, 45**, and descending with **54, 43, 32**). Substituting fingers frequently occurs in double-note passages such as 10C. Just try the upper voice, holding the low E with the thumb, with fingers **5, 4, 3, 2**, and then try playing the penultimate C with either **3, 4,** or **5** and see what happens. Finger substitution will prevent the unnecessary stretching and cramping you probably just experienced and can be executed very rapidly once you get the hang of it. Finger substitutions are indicated in the fingering.

Fingering can also be used to ensure articulation.

EXAMPLE 11

As discussed above, one should read the dots in Example 11 as rests. If you use the second finger on C and D you have to make the rest required by the dot. The same is true after the F, and the rest is guaranteed by using the fourth finger on F and E. The articulation is built into the fingering and you do not have to think about it any more – it will always be there. Although such fingering is not essential, there are times it will get you out of a tangle as you will see throughout the fingerings for these sonatas.

In sequences the fingering is given for the basic motif but not for its repetitions on different pitches if the fingering remains the same. Any change in fingering necessitated by accidentals is given.

When a phrase is repeated the fingering is given only the first time.

## The Instrument

By now you have probably begun wondering what instrument I am discussing: the harpsichord or the piano. Both! What works on one instrument works on the other.

Scarlatti, of course, wrote for the harpsichord and for that reason the sonatas sound best on that instrument, and the preceding discussions have admittedly been based on its technique. There is no reason, however, why the sonatas should not be played on the piano. Certain Baroque composers, Couperin for instance, wrote so idiomatically for the harpsichord that it is impossible to transfer the music to the piano without losing a great deal of its effect. This is not true of Scarlatti. Like Bach's music for the harpsichord, Scarlatti's sonatas are of such musical worth that they transcend the original instrument and are tremendously effective on either the harpsichord or the piano. There is no need to apologise for playing them on the piano as is attested by the wonderful performances of such pianists as Vladimir Horowitz or Alicia de Larrocha. But the fact still remains that they were written for the harpsichord and for that reason it is essential that anyone playing them on the piano be aware of the musical properties of the harpsichord.

Many pianists will undoubtedly object to my limiting the use of the wrists to phrasing. They will say that the wrist is essential to produce a fine tone on the piano and that the wrist technique given above makes that impossible. While this is true for the romantic repertory of the nineteenth-century, especially in the works of Chopin, Liszt and Brahms where the hand is constantly spread out for octaves and chords and accompanying figures are spun out over several octaves, it is not necessarily true for the Baroque and classical repertory of the eighteenth century. Harpsichord composers, and even such composers as Haydn and Mozart writing for the fortepiano, wrote so that the fingers were kept close to each other. Their passage work did not require a spread hand. In this close position the player could produce sufficient tone simply by raising the finger and striking it down firmly. The wrist (and arm and shoulders, for that matter) were not needed to produce the opulent tone the romantic masters required. The music was filled with minute articulations which in the Baroque era were not carefully written out but which are painstakingly indicated in the works of the early piano composers. The wrist was free to phrase and the fingers left to define the articulation.

In the nineteenth century the thickness of the writing required more tone and the hand was spread out to reach the notes. The wrist gradually lost its function of phrasing and was used to produce a beautiful tone as more weight was applied to the keyboard. The articulation so dear to the eighteenth century was lost, and a long legato line moulded by dynamic expression replaced the lost articulation.

One of the best examples of what happens when the wrist is used simultaneously to produce tone and to articulate is seen in the very first *allegro* in the first movement of Beethoven's 'Tempest' Sonata, Op.31, No.3. After a slow arpeggiated figure, Beethoven introduces a rapid passage based on a series of two-note slurs beginning:

EXAMPLE 12

I was instructed, as many of us were and still are to this day, to use a separate wrist action for each two notes. No matter how many times I practised it that way the passage was never really secure. In the extended version of the same passage which occurs in the recapitulation, I usually jammed up along the way and rarely got through it. Years later, after I had shifted my loyalties to the harpsichord, but not so completely that I ignored the piano entirely, I returned to the 'Tempest' and tried using my wrist to phrase the passage and let my fingers take care of the articulation. I have never had trouble with that passage since. It proved to me without a shadow of doubt that, even on the piano, reserving the wrist for phrasing and the fingers for articulation works. Good fingers are perfectly capable of producing all the tone that is required to play Baroque and classical music on the piano. Any attempt to enrich that tone by means of the wrist simply eliminates the articulation which is such a part and parcel of eighteenth-century keyboard music. Therefore, the technique described above of using the wrist for the phrase and fingers for articulation works, perforce, just as well on the piano as it does on the harpsichord. The only way to believe it is to try it.

But, cries the pianist, what about dynamics? Try working with temporal expression for a while. Once the use of rubato along with articulation and touch becomes part of your musical language, the dynamics will take care of themselves. Certainly the pianist will use dynamics, but not logically until he first thinks temporally. If you think of dynamics first, you put the cart before the horse and are apt to superimpose dynamics on a piece which are inappropriate and sound artificial. Scarlatti had no recourse to dynamics, and yet he certainly must have been an expressive player to write such poetic music.

And, objects the harpsichordist, you speak of accents to set off the beginning of an articulation. It is impossible to make an accent on the harpsichord. This is not entirely true. It is, of course, possible to make a far more pronounced accent on the piano than it is on the harpsichord, but one can make a slight accent on it. More important than the actual accent, is the thought of it. Just thinking about it will set a note off.

What about the pedal? The soul of the piano! There is no reason to refrain from using the pedal. In fact there is nothing more appalling than hearing a pianist play Baroque music or Haydn and Mozart without pedal. But start out learning a piece without it. This will ensure that your fingers create the legato and slurs. Using the pedal for such purposes is not only a cheat but also smears the melodic line and clouds the harmonies. Then add a touch of the pedal for coloration.

The piano is a magnificent instrument and it has its own characteristics which should not be suppressed. There is nothing more arid, in fact, than a pianist trying to imitate the harpsichord or a pianist playing the harpsichord like a piano. But the pianist playing harpsichord music on the piano, unlike a harpsichordist playing harpsichord music on the harpsichord, must be aware of the inherent nature of the harpsichord. Once he is aware of it, which he will be after studying the sonatas as suggested in this edition, he will then be fully prepared to play 'pianistically' without losing the inherent nature of the music. For this reason I have deliberately avoided any reference to a specific instrument. The technique and style presented above will work very well on either the harpsichord or the piano.

## Sources

This edition is based on: Domenico Scarlatti, *Complete Keyboard Works in Facsimile from the Manuscript and Printed Sources*, edited by Ralph Kirkpatrick (New York and London: Johnson Reprint Corporation, 1972). Referring to Kirkpatrick as the editor is somewhat misleading in that he has not actually edited the music but rather has selected and reproduced what he considered to be the most reliable sources from the earliest printed editions and manuscripts. He has also arranged them in what he believed to be as close to chronological order as possible. Anyone seeking more information about this matter is referred to the preface of the above or Kirkpatrick's excellent biography of Scarlatti (Princeton, New Jersey: Princeton University Press, 1953). His detailed section on ornamentation is also of particular interest.

*Ringoes, New Jersey, 1988*  **Stoddard Lincoln**

## Table of signs and ornaments

Notes with dots over them are to be played detached or staccato.

Notes under a slur are to be overlapped.

All other notes are played legato, i.e. joined but not overlapped. They may be imperceptibly detached in brilliant passages.

Square brackets indicate phrases and are to be taken with one rising-wrist motion.

Commas indicate articulations and are to be made with the fingers only within the rising-wrist motion of the phrase.

Appoggiaturas are slurred to the note they precede, i.e. the two notes are overlapped. All appoggiaturas are taken on the beat, and the time value, indicated by the appoggiatura itself, is to be subtracted from the note of resolution. The duration of an appoggiatura may be lengthened or shortened at the discretion of the player.

Acciaccaturas are indicated by a grace note with a slash through it. They are to be played as quickly as possible if not 'smashed', i.e. played simultaneously with the note they precede.

The short trill (⁀) is taken on the beat, not before, and takes less than the value of the note when possible so that there is a pause before the next note. It may begin on the principal note or the upper auxiliary at the discretion of the player. The fingering will suggest the editor's preference. If the short trill is preceded by a grace note above it, the trill *must* begin on the upper auxiliary. All such grace notes are Scarlatti's, not the editor's.

The long trill (**tr**) is also taken on the beat but lasts the entire value of the note and ends with a turn, i.e. the last note of the trill will be one note lower than the trill and will go directly without pause to the next note. They too may begin on the principal note or upper auxiliary (editorial preference indicated by the fingering) unless preceded by a grace note on the upper auxiliary. Short and long trills are interchangeable at the player's discretion unless there is a written termination (Scarlatti's, not the editor's), in which case a long trill with the written termination *must* be used.

For a fuller explanation of the above, see the editor's *Preface* in Volume One. Details concerning specific passages are found in the editor's commentary that precedes each set.

## Notes on the individual sonatas: Volume One

### Set 1 in F Major
*1. K. 274 (L. 297)*
This march-like sonata will introduce curious scales in contrary motion, strengthen trills and present double notes. Take it rather pompously.

*bb 11–13* This and similar passages can easily be turned into trill exercises by extending the trill of the second beat a full measure.

EXAMPLE 1

*bb 14–17* All the contrary scale passages are to be slurred in order to contrast with the rest of the piece. The articulation between the slurs, made with your fingers, not wrists, is almost imperceptible. In the second half, beginning at bar 37, crossing the 3rd finger over the 4th where indicated will ensure this break.

*2. K. 85 (L. 166)*
This somewhat frenzied sonata, not written in the usual binary structure, will get your fingers working with its scales and arpeggios and rattling left hand. Begin practising it slowly and gradually work up to the suggested tempo, and use a metronome as this piece has a way of rushing. You will want to return to it frequently as a warm-up. Don't be afraid to increase the speed to more than 112 when you can.

The basic articulation for the entire piece is found in the first bar: three semiquavers used as an upbeat to four quavers, two slurred and two staccato. The upbeat figure must always be articulated even when it appears in the midst of semiquavers as in bar 2. A clean break will halt the flow of the semiquavers, so just give it an accent which will mark it.

Beginning in bar 20, the upbeat scale is intervallically augmented to an arpeggio (see bars 25–28 and following) and must be given the same articulation.

The first bar also gives rise to the articulation in the left hand for bar 3 and similar passages. The right-hand figure in bar 4 could also take the same articulation by placing staccatos on the second two quavers, but the effect is rather too choppy over the noisy left hand. The two slurred quavers of the right hand manage to subdue it a bit.

*b 25* Remember that the first note after a tie is read as a rest, otherwise you will get into trouble with the fingering in bars 27 and 28.

# THE SCHOLAR'S SCARLATTI
## VOLUME ONE

Edited by
Stoddard Lincoln

Domenico SCARLATTI
(1685 - 1757)

a. [Set 1, F major]
### 1. K. 274; L. 297

© Copyright 1989 Novello & Company Limited

All Rights Reserved

3

## 2. K. 85; L. 166

**Allegro** ♩=112

5

**Set 2 in G major**

*3. K. 289 (L. 78)*
This crisp sonata will continue your work in short arpeggios and scales in parallel and contrary motion. Its tonal architecture is curious: rather than making the usual modulation to the dominant in the first half it goes to B minor, the relative minor of the dominant.

Note the articulation of the first two bars carefully: a quaver and two semiquavers followed by two staccato quavers. These figures appear throughout the sonata and are consistently articulated that way. Always set the semiquavers into motion with a slight accent.

The scale figure introduced at bar 11 should be played legato whenever it occurs in order to offer contrast with the opening idea.

*bb 40–44*  In order to hold the B with the thumb it is necessary to indulge in some finger crossing.

*bb 45 & 69*  A quaver note followed by two semiquavers preceded by a short appoggiatura is usually played as four semiquavers. Such a reading, however, does not apply to Scarlatti and would destroy the prevalent anapaest rhythm of the piece, so play the grace note as an acciaccatura.

*b 70*  Really work at these trills between the 3rd and 4th fingers. They begin on the upper auxiliary and Scarlatti has indicated a termination. This ornament is ubiquitous in Baroque music and an indispensable part of one's technique. If you cannot manage it at the moment and still wish to enjoy the sonata, play the upper auxiliary as an acciaccatura followed by two semiquavers which is in keeping with bars 45 and 69. But remember, this is only a temporary easy way out until you have mastered a good 3rd- and 4th-finger trill.

*bb 80–81*  There is no reason why you can't play the trill in bar 80 with your 2nd and 3rd fingers but why not be masochistic and use the 3rd and 4th in order to strengthen them?

In bar 81 don't worry about the exact rhythm yet. If you play all the notes on the first beat as a sextuplet the effect will be very good. When this is secure try the written rhythm.

*4. K. 35 (L. 386)*
This Handelian-sounding sonata extends semiquaver passage work considerably and strengthens the 4th and 5th fingers.

*bb 1–3*  The articulations between the first and second semiquavers in both hands should be very slight so as not to disturb the flow of the passages involved. A slight accent on the semiquaver after the articulation should suffice.

Keep a high wrist for the quavers in the left hand so that you can move smoothly from the thumb to the 5th finger in bar 3. Don't try to pass the 5th finger over but merely move the hand to its new position in one quick motion. There will be a break which is stylistically correct and the constantly rising wrist will keep the phrase. Practise it thus:

EXAMPLE 2

*bb 8–11*  While the thumb of the left hand reiterates a pedal point D on the second and fourth semiquavers, the first and third notes should form a legato line. This is known as 'finger-pedalling' and should be practised:

EXAMPLE 3

*bb 12–15*  Beginning on the third beat the right hand is scored for two voices. Be sure to play them legato observing the fingering carefully so that the suspensions are heard.

*bb 15–17*  This can be turned into a good trill exercise by practising it as follows:

EXAMPLE 4

Apply the same exercise to bar 38 and the last two beats of bars 35 and 36. The latter will really put steel into your 4th and 5th fingers!

*b 38*   The crotchets in the left hand should probably be played quavers followed by quaver rests as is written out in bar 17.

## 5. K. 425 (L. 333)

This sonata will introduce Scarlatti's Spanish style and get you into some leaps and double notes as well as a real Scarlattian finger-twister at the crux.

*b 1*   The two-note figure in the left hand should end with a very sharp staccato. The slur implies that the first note should be held until the second is released. This articulation should be consistent throughout the work wherever the figure appears.

*bb 49 – 65*   With patience the right hand will fall into place. In order to measure the placement of the 4th and 5th fingers, try holding the thumb down on the A. Be sure to observe the left-hand articulation as it gives the passage its life. The same goes for the crux.

*bb 70 – 73 & 78 – 81*   This fingering keeps the thumb off the accidentals. The staccato articulation is somewhat arbitrary but it works with a slight ritardando before the fermata. Concerning fermatas: in general one makes a slight ritardando before them. The ritardando is even broader if the fermata is over a measure's rest as in bar 106.

*bb 99 – 106*   This is a very difficult passage indeed, but practised slowly it will improve your double-note technique greatly. Scarlatti calls for a trill in bar 105 which taxes the best technique. Although Scarlatti never used the mordent it is possible to use one here effectively (D – C sharp – D) which I have indicated in the score. Also helpful is taking the final D of the right hand with the left-hand thumb making sure that one hangs on to the low D with the 5th finger. The use of a ritardando will also make this passage possible.

b. [Set 2, G major]
## 3. K. 289; L. 78

7

# 4. K. 35; L. 386

9

# 5. K. 425; L. 333

11

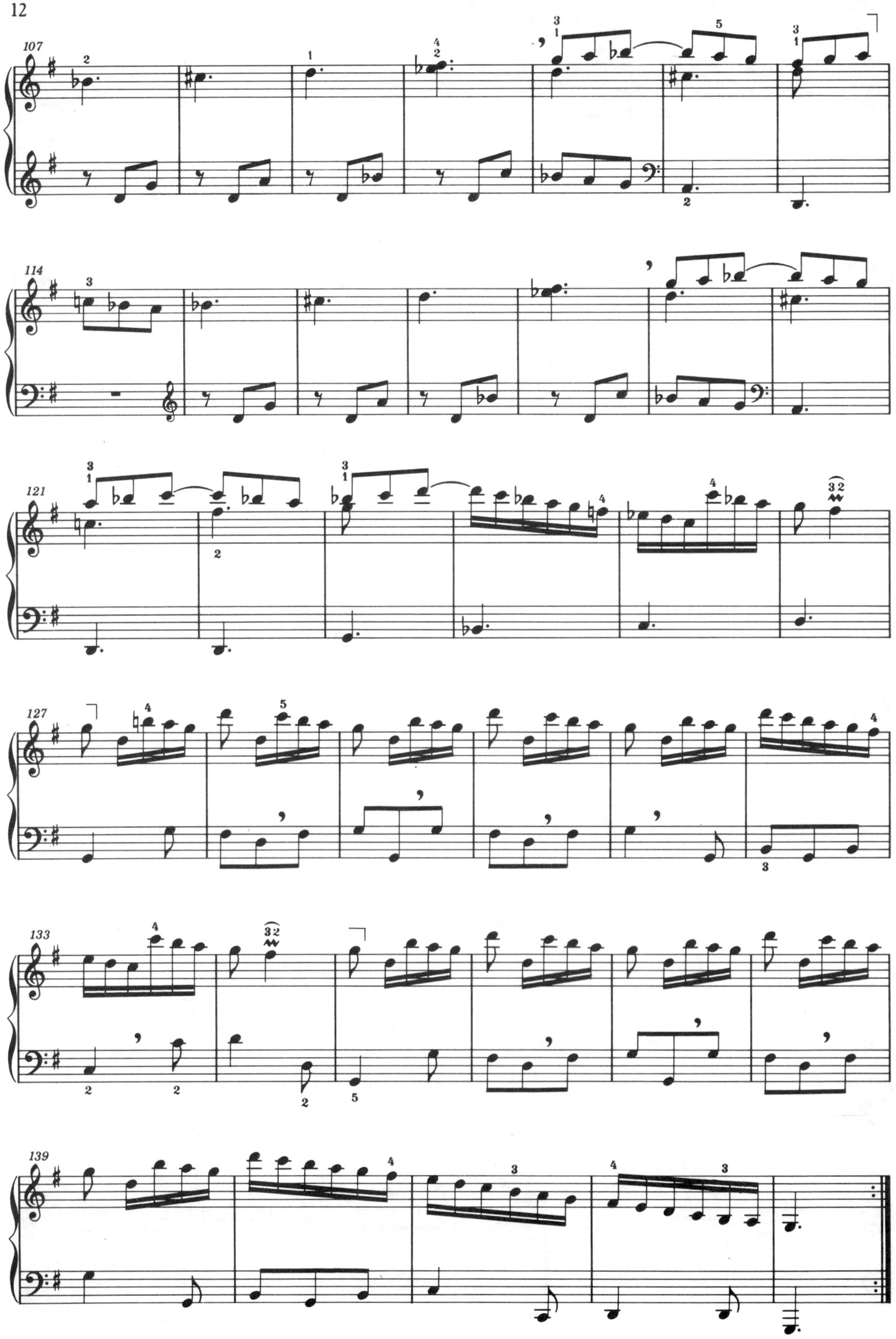

**Set 3 in D Major**

*6. K. 335 (LS.10)*
This sonata is very good for physically feeling out the size of various intervals with the hand such as the fourths in bars 15 and 16, the sixths in 28 – 30, and the octave filled in with a third beginning in bar 43.
*bb 18 – 19* The D-minor arpeggio is slurred in order to mark the sudden change to the minor. Note that the slur is applied only to the arpeggio and that there is the slightest break before taking the 2nd finger over to the F. This use of a break (but always within one wrist movement) is frequently used to emphasize a downbeat which is preceded by a quicker upbeat and should be used every time this figure occurs in the sonata.

Notice that bar 18 through to the first beat of bar 28 makes up two phrases. The rests in the right hand give the articulations. At first one might use a separate wrist movement for each articulation, i.e. for bars 19 – 20, then bars 21 – 22, etc. Ultimately, however, you will want to take each entire phrase with one wrist movement which includes the rests. By so doing, the two-bar fragments will be held together in one large unit which will keep the constant forward motion of the music as opposed to the stop and go feeling you will create if you take separate wrists for each fragment.

*7. K. 333 (L. 269)*
This sonata is unusual in that the first and second sections are completely different from each other. Although an exact rhythmic ratio between the two sections is not necessary, a steady pulse can be maintained throughout the entire work if the minim of the first section is equal to the dotted crotchet of the second section. Let the basic pulse be governed by how quickly you can play the second half, and then use that tempo for the first half.
*b 23* This passage is excellent for the stretch between the 2nd and 4th fingers. The thumb will keep your hand in position and, when it is not there, pretend that it is. If your hand is small get off the C sharp quickly. Trying to hold it might injure your hand. (Remember what happened to Robert Schumann, and he adored Scarlatti.)
*b 42* Scarlatti's second ending begins at bar 42 with the repeat sign before the low A in the left hand and there is no A in the right hand. One questions the accuracy of this reading for two reasons: 1) The scale in bars 39 and 40 demands a final A as is given in the first ending. Leaving it out for the second ending makes no sense at all; 2) The low A in the second ending cadences the first half, and the subject for the second half begins with the ascending scale for the left hand beginning on the second beat of the second ending. Placing the repeat sign after the second beat of the second ending solves this problem and is also consistent with the fact that there is no rest after the final dotted crotchet in Scarlatti's original.
*bb 48 – 49* Although using the thumb on all of the upper notes of the left hand is awkward, it is the only fingering that works at a quick tempo. Try it by practising Example 5A keeping the wrist high. Then try Example 5B keeping the thumb as flexible as possible.

EXAMPLE 5

*bb 52 – 62* However much one may be tempted to make more use of the thumb in the right hand of this passage, this fingering is designed to use it as little as possible in order to keep the hand relaxed. For example, it would seem logical to use the thumb in the second beat of bar 52 (**2 – 1 – 2 – 1**) and in similar passages. This, however, locks the thumb under the second finger and can cause stiffness which will hinder the flow of the passage.
*b 67* The original A on the first beat for the left hand makes no harmonic sense. Compare with the first beat of bar 72.

*8. K. 77 (L. 168)*
This early composition is really a short two-movement sonata laid out in a typically Baroque format: a slow first movement followed by a quicker dance, in this case a Minuet. It is essential in this sonata that you observe the Baroque articulation of ties and rests, otherwise the fingering, which takes this

articulation into account, will not work. To recapitulate: read all dots as rests and the second note of a tie as a rest.

EXAMPLE 6

Such a reading takes care of the articulation in this piece automatically and I have therefore not indicated it with the usual comma.

Notice that there are only four phrases in the entire first movement and in order not to turn each articulation into a short phrase, which will destroy the long line of the music, it is essential to use the wrist properly. This is a good time to concentrate on that problem and I suggest that you practise as follows. Looking at the prevalent articulation beginning at bar 3, you will observe that each unit consists of seven semiquavers (really eight, but the first one after a tie is read as a rest, as is written out in bar 13). The last note of the run, in almost all cases, is repeated as a short appoggiatura to the crotchet which begins the next bar. In order to ensure that the appoggiatura is clearly heard, I have indicated a change of finger for the last note of the run and the appoggiatura. Begin by taking the second two beats of bar 3 and the first beat of bar 4 in a single wrist. (Be sure not to use a wrist for the appoggiatura, but take with your finger.) After a few tries, move on to the next unit (bars 4 and 5), then on to bars 5 and 6 and so on. Notice that the run is extended in bars 11 and 12 and that there is no appoggiatura. This also happens at bars 15 and 16 and a trill is included. After you have mastered each of these units on a separate wrist go back and take two units on one wrist, (bars 3–5, 5–7 etc.). When you go through the movements this way try three units at a time then four. Now you can take the phrasing as indicated with as many articulations as required within the rising motion of one wrist. This admittedly tries one's patience, but the results are well worth the effort. It will instill into you the distinction between articulation and phrasing. If such a distinction is not made the music is shapeless, lacks direction and, worse, becomes boring.

All of the slurs are Scarlatti's and although they are not placed over all of the semiquavers, it seems obvious that he intends them all to be slurred (compare bar 12 with bar 40). In any event *legatississimo* is the word of the day.

*b 31* Use a 3rd-and-4th-finger trill here if you have it and avoid the awkward leap between **2** and **5**. Treat the B and A as a termination in demi-semiquavers. The concept of a double dot was unknown in Scarlatti's day, otherwise he would have written as follows:

EXAMPLE 7

This matches up with the demi-semiquaver note termination in bar 32 which he can write properly because only a single dot is required.

*b 37* This is the climax of the piece and you might try a little rubato here. Begin the run slowly with a slight accelerando to the E flat. The E flat implies the expressive Neapolitan sixth, and in order to bring it out linger on it ever so slightly. In other words, fool around with this passage so that it takes on a special expressiveness, bearing in mind that it must be subtly done and not so exaggerated that it destroys the basic pulse.

*Minuet* The slurs in the left hand are editorial and, in order to give the piece a dance-like lilt, hold the first note slightly. Also, as in the preceding piece, the phrases are very long; there are only two in fact so that the short runs before the appoggiaturas must be treated as articulations.

Spend hours and hours with this unassuming little sonata as mastery of its articulation and phrasing will work wonders in your playing and you will come out an excellent musician.

*b 62* G on the third beat in the original.

*b 71* Final semiquaver is C in the original.

## 9. K. 178 (L. 162)

This perky little sonata makes a perfect close to this set and also gets you into some nice leaping of octaves.

*(Notes to Set 3 continue on p. xxiv)*

## c. [Set 3, D major]
# 6. K. 335; L.S. 10

14

15

# 7. K. 333; L. 269

17

# 8. K. 77; L. 168

**Moderato e cantabile** ♩ = 72

19

## 9. K. 178; L. 162

21

*bb 1 & 2* The trill between the B and C sharp is awkward at best. For practical purposes I suggest that you begin it on the principal note unless, of course, you have developed that fabulous 3rd-and-4th-finger trill by now. If you find it too difficult beginning on the principal note, don't give the piece up; simply play a C-sharp acciaccatura. But whatever your solution is, play all the trills of this figure throughout the next thirteen bars the same way!

*bb 30-40* Use the thumb on the first C sharp if you *must* but it is cheating. Eventually you must be able to jump around between fingers other than **1** and **5**. Just look at the last three bars if you don't believe it.

**Set 4 in C Major**
*10. K. 165 (L.52)*
This lyric sonata is typical of Scarlatti's writing in the 'Gallant' style. Gallant melodies are characterised by their use of many different rhythmic values (in this case the values include minims, crotchets, quavers, triplets and semiquavers) and wide leaps. These supple melodies are supported by the simplest bass line which frequently uses repeated notes.

The rhythms of the melody must be played exactly and it is especially important to be able to move smoothly between duplets, triplets and semiquavers without altering the underlying pulse. Since this is easier said than done, you might try the following exercise away from the keyboard to test yourself. Set your metronome to a moderate crotchet pulse and feel it in 2/4. Then, using the syllable 'ta', try moving up from crotchets, quavers, triplets, to semiquavers and back.

EXAMPLE 8

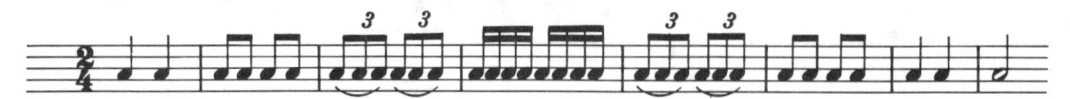

You will find it more difficult moving from the quicker values to the slower ones than *vice versa*. When you can do this easily, turn the metronome off and tap a steady beat with your right hand performing the 'ta's' over that. The most difficult passage in this sonata rhythmically is bars 46 – 50 where the differentiation between duplets and triplets is compounded by the use of syncopation plus repeated notes which require changing fingers. Notice in bars 46 and 47 that I have put in an articulation mark which serves to delay the last quaver of each bar. This brings out the syncopation and turns what might be a mechanical reading into an expressive one. Always remember that this is to be done on one wrist.

Once you can play this at a steady tempo with the metronome you will want to use some rubato in order to bring out the expressive qualities of some of the leaps and unusual harmonies. In bars 18 to 22, for example, there are some wide leaps and very expressive harmonies. Take a little time for the first note of bar 19, more time for the first note of bar 20 (the fingering will force you to do this), and then linger on the first note of bar 21 and hold down the first four quavers of the melody (as the slur implies) so that we can savour the diminished seventh chord which resolves in bar 22. Then return to tempo, making sure that the triplets of the right hand are in exact proportion to the duplets in the left hand.

You will also want to measure the leap to the first note of bar 28, but not too much as this happens again in bar 32 where you will want to take more time. The last beat of bar 34 and first beat of bar 35 also require time and even more time when the passage is repeated. Never repeat a passage exactly the same; hint at rubato the first time and then really apply it the second. Feel free to experiment with rubato but only after you can play what is written in exact time. Never let it become too exaggerated as it will sound gross and destroy the basic underlying beat and, again, always keep the wrist in motion to get to the end of the phrase!

The left-hand accompaniment is not as easy as it seems and it would be well to play it alone in order to explore its melodic nature. Keep it legato and smooth. The repeated notes must be treated very specially so that they do not become too detached from each other and sound bumpy. In bars 11 and 12, for example, don't let your finger leave the B flat. Just let the key rise enough so that you can retake it clearly with no space between the notes. Imagine a cello taking all three notes on the same bow. There is scarcely any space between them but the pulse is heard because of pressure. The same technique must be applied to the repeated double notes that open the second half of the movement. This technique of retaking repeated notes smoothly is difficult and will not work unless you take them within the phrase with that constantly-rising wrist. If the wrist technique is ignored, the accompaniment will be obtrusive and obscure the melody of the right hand.

*bb 54 & 55*  Do not disturb the triplet rhythm by playing the ornament too slowly, and be careful that they do not turn into quavers followed by two semiquavers as in bars 52 and 53. If you have trouble here substitute an upper-neighbour acciaccatura for the trill.

The slurs in bar 26 and wherever that figure appears throughout the piece are Scarlatti's. He also indicated slurs in bars 42 and 44. The rest are editorial.

## 11. K. 255 (L. 439)

This sonata is excellent for octaves filled in with various other notes, and double notes.

*bb 5 & 6*  Here is a case where crossing the 3rd finger over the 4th will ensure the articulation.

*bb 9–32*  Do not slap the right hand wrist to make it easier to play this octave figure. As usual, start with a low wrist which will gradually rise according to the phrasing and use the fingers to get the octaves.

*b 37 Oytabado*  Perhaps a dance? The term is unknown. Follow the above advice given for bars 13–32 in playing this passage as a flailing wrist will produce a choppy effect and also jeopardize the accuracy.

*bb 64–80 Tortorilla.*  To do with doves – perhaps their cooing? Although not marked as such the articulation and fingering of the left hand will produce a hemiola which lasts until the double bar. Be sure to hold the thumb for two beats in order to ensure the slur.

*bb 118–121*  At best the trill here is awkward. The best expediency is to use a turn even though it is uncalled for.

EXAMPLE 9

If this causes trouble (after having given it a chance, of course), simply omit the ornament altogether and add it at some later date.

**Set 5 in A Major**

*12. K. 300 (L. 92)*
This charming sonata is classical sounding with its graceful motivic work, flowing accompaniment figures and symmetrical phrasing. It should be played smoothly with lots of legato.

*bb 1–6*   These bars and the opening of the second section are a rare example of Scarlatti's use of imitative counterpoint. In order to ensure the independence of the two contrapuntal lines, practise them hands separately following the articulation precisely before you put them together.

In bar 4, and in similar passages, crossing the 3rd finger over the 4th in the left hand gives a smoother line than would a fingering which passes the thumb under.

*bb 7 & 8*   Finger-pedal the left hand. That is, play the quavers that fall on the beat as legato crotchets. This accompanying figure appears frequently during the piece and should always be finger-pedalled.

*b 11*   Finger-pedal the left hand as much as you can.

*bb 21–3*   Try to get some variety in this triple repetition by toying with the trill. You might begin the first one on the main note and play it evenly. Begin the second one the same way but linger on the first note. Then play the last one beginning on the upper auxiliary. There are many possibilities so experiment. The articulation between the trill and the triplet is to ensure that the ornament comes to a stop before going into the triplet rather than going into it directly as though it were a termination.

*bb 26–35*   The right-hand slurs in bars 26–30 are Scarlatti's; the rest are editorial. He obviously wants it very legato in contrast to the preceding section. Try some expressive rubato here. You might hold the first note of bar 28 to prepare for the entry of the left hand and the same in bar 31. Certainly take time to get to the high D in bar 32. It is the climax of the passage because it is approached by the widest leap and is also the highest note. Don't be afraid to take rhythmic liberties.

Although it is not necessary to begin the trill in bar 34 on the upper auxiliary, doing so emphasizes the dissonance, F sharp and C. Take the ornament slowly in preparation for the suggested fermata, playing the appoggiatura as a quaver, and go on *a tempo* after a slight pause.

*bb 41–45*   The last four bars are an extension of the phrase beginning at bar 36, so try to take it from there on one wrist. A crotchet D-sharp appoggiatura to the final E is appropriate if you wish to add it. Try a G-sharp appoggiatura for the final cadence at bar 90. If you take the repeats in this sonata, leave out the suggested appoggiaturas the first time around and add them for variety in the repetition.

*b 65*   In repeated-note accompaniments do not break two-note chords, but when there are three-note chords break them slightly to soften their effect. In bar 65 break the first chord more than the second two as it emphasizes the unusual use of a 4/2 harmony here.

*bb 68 & 80*   Beginning this trill with the thumb may seem awkward at first but it is the only way to ensure a legato from the preceding note. Take your time crossing over from the thumb to the 3rd finger and then quicken the rest of the ornament.

*bb 74–80*   The slurs in this passage are Scarlatti's; the rest in this section are editorial. It is parallel to bars 26–35 in the first section and you should experiment with some rubato here as you did there. Certainly take your time at the highest note and gradually work back to tempo, pausing before continuing at bar 81. This passage, incidentally, is excellent for contractions. Practise it slowly at first feeling out the distance between each interval.

*13. K. 285 (L. 91)*
Similar in its classical phrasing and motivic work to the preceding sonata, this perky little piece makes a fine contrast. Building on one motif, Scarlatti ingeniously manipulates it with great wit.

The motif, found in the first bar, must always be articulated the same way by the use of a staccato on the fourth beat. The staccato must be produced with your finger, not wrist. At bar 29 Scarlatti has you hold down your little finger for the entire bar, a requirement which makes it impossible to use the wrist for the fourth-beat staccato. Try those measures first to get the gesture and then begin the piece.

*b 19*   No matter what you do with this bar, it is a mess. In the first place, one wonders how the quavers got there as they are the only ones in the left hand found in the entire piece. The F sharp is only an accented passing note to the E and would not be missed.

EXAMPLE 10A

This would certainly help matters. Here is another solution which I certainly recommend even though it is a blatant cheat:

EXAMPLE 10B

*14. K. 149 (L. 93)*
Scarlatti was the first composer to recommend changing fingers on repeated notes and this sonata faces that problem head on. In bar 6 there are eight repeated notes; these are to be played with the fingering indicated and the same way whenever they appear even though only the placement of the initial 4th finger is given. Scarlatti marks them here and in the next bar with a staccato which is hardly necessary if you have ever tried to play repeated notes at this tempo legato.

d. [Set 4, C major]
# 10. K. 165; L. 52

23

# 11. K. 255; L. 439

25

e. [Set 5, A major]
## 12. K. 300; L. 92

27

28

# 13. K. 285; L. 91

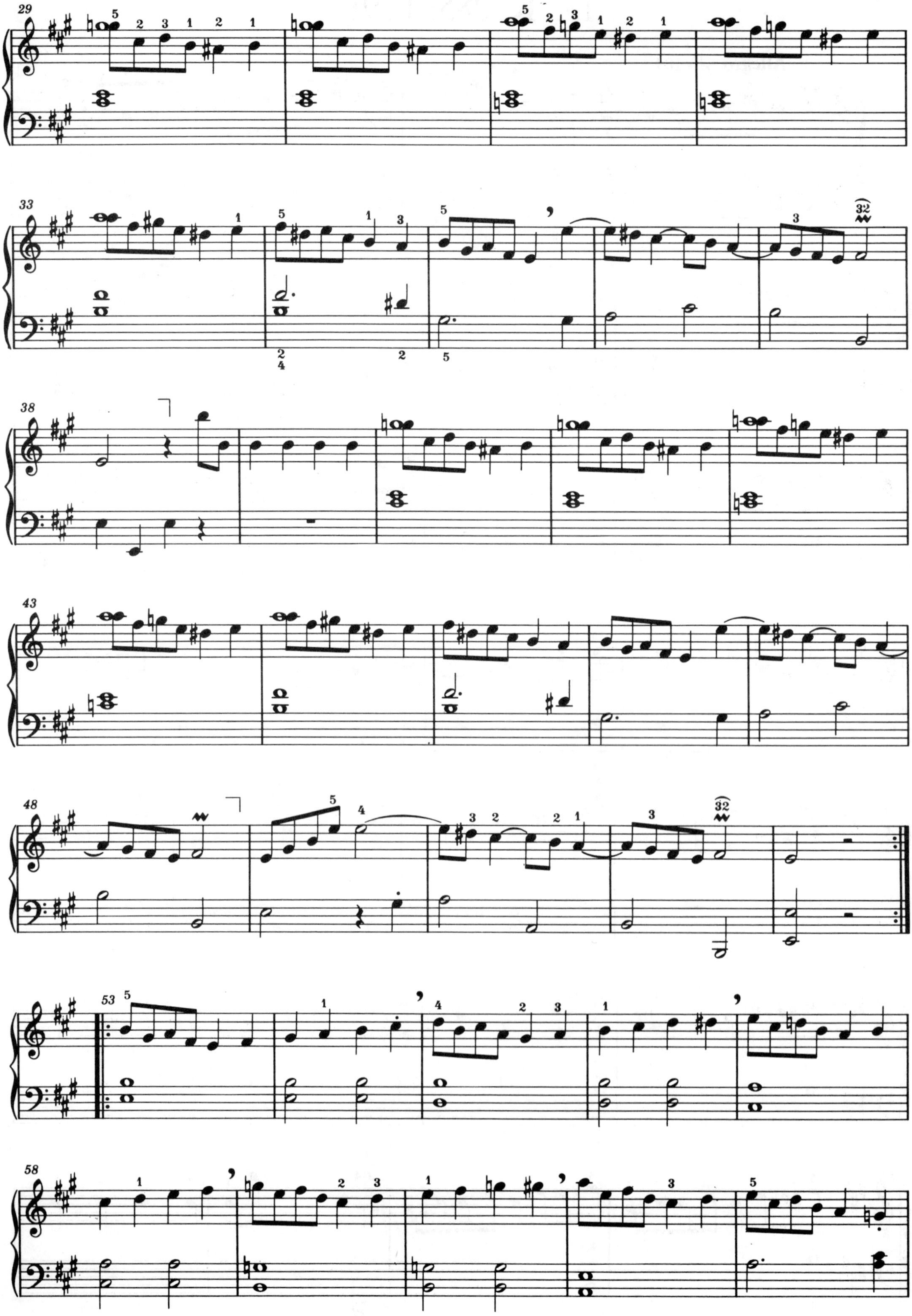
29
33
38
43
48
53
58

31

# 14. K. 149; L. 93

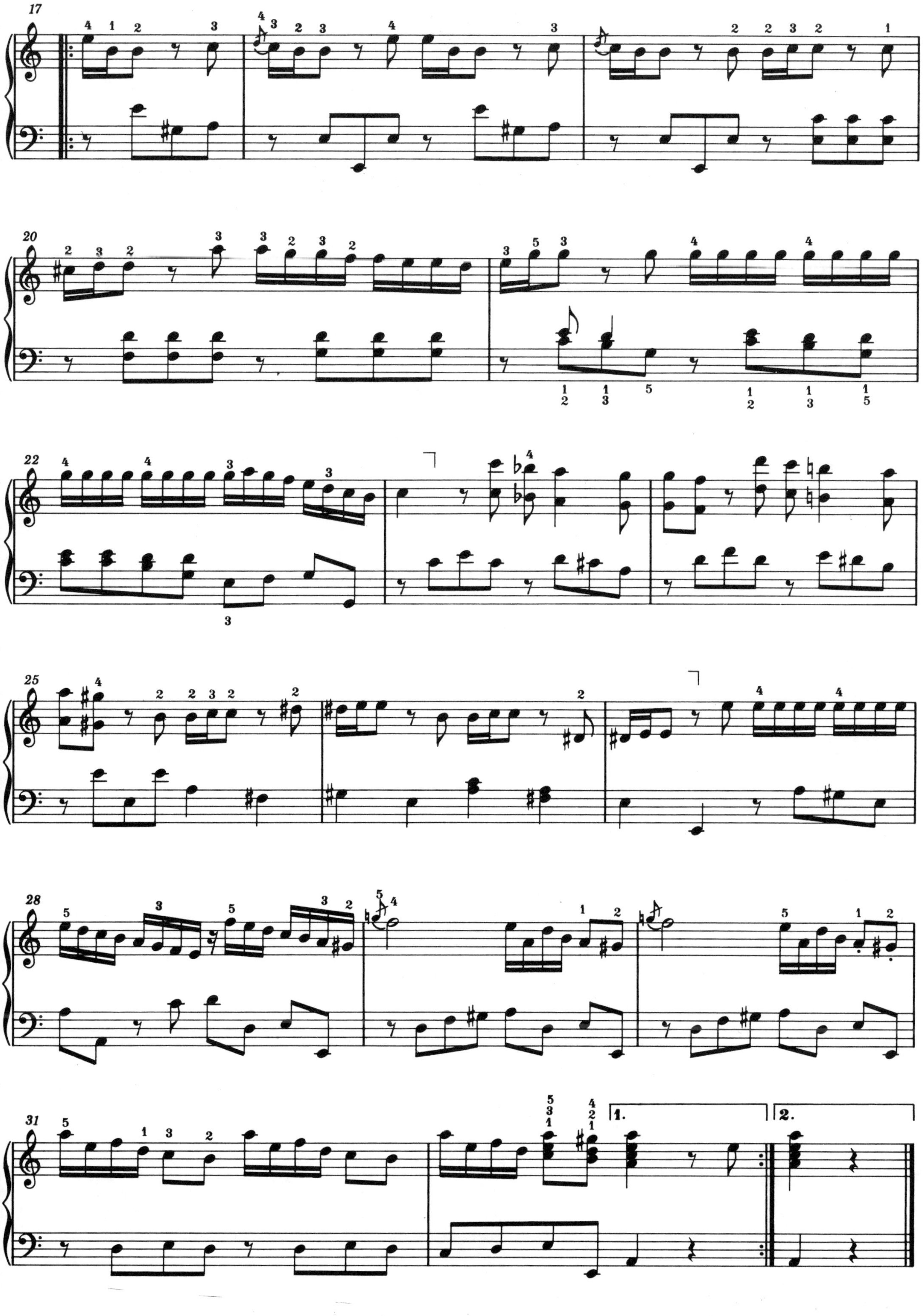

2/04(49605)
Printed in England